WRITING CHANGES EVERYTHING

WRITING CHANGES EVERYTHING

Edited by Deborah Brodie

THE 627 BEST THINGS
ANYONE EVER SAID
ABOUT WRITING

ST. MARTIN'S PRESS
NEW YORK

Grateful acknowledgment is made for permission to reprint excerpts from "Eating Poetry," from *Reasons for Moving* by Mark Strand (Alfred A. Knopf, Inc.), copyright © 1968 by Mark Strand and "The Greatdog Poems," first published in *The New Yorker,* © 1996 by Mark Strand. Used by permission of the author.

Design by Songhee Kim
Illustrations by Michael Storrings

Library of Congress Cataloging-in-Publication Data

Writing changes everything : the 627 best things anyone ever said
    about writing / Deborah Brodie, editor.
        p.   cm.
    Includes index.
    ISBN 0-312-15432-1
        1. Authorship–Quotations, maxims, etc.   2. Authors–Quotations.
    I. Brodie, Deborah.
    PN165.W76   1997
    808'.02–dc21   96-40453
                                                             CIP

First Edition: May 1997

1   3   5   7   9   10   8   6   4   2

I have forced myself to begin writing when I've been utterly exhausted, when I've felt my soul as thin as a playing card . . . and somehow the activity of writing changes everything.

JOYCE CAROL OATES

Acknowledgments

"There are three rules for writing a novel," said W. Somerset Maugham. "Unfortunately no one knows what they are." Perhaps he would have found the answer had he talked to my dynamic and perceptive agent, Carla M. Glasser. Or my dedicated editor, Marian Lizzi, whose insights I greatly appreciate. Or my colleague and friend, Lisa Bernstein, whose commentary has helped make this book a reality.

I am grateful to Claire M. Smith and Barbara Anderson, who first "saw the angel in the marble"; my friends at the Society of Children's Book Writers and Illustrators, especially Lin Oliver, Stephen Mooser, and—for her enthusiasm—Sue Alexander.

I want to thank my publishing colleagues who are also wise and giving friends: Francesca Belanger, Judy Carey, Janet Pascal, and, especially, Sandee Brawarsky and Judith Herschlag Muffs. Also (sometimes it takes a village to make a book), Ann A. Flowers, Patricia Reilly Giff, Louis Phillips,

Michael Storrings, Mark Strand, Burton L. Visotzky, and my students in the Writing Program at the New School. And Regina Hayes for her unwavering support and her expertise, both literary and sartorial—here's to the next fifteen years!

Thank you to Kenneth David Burrows, Helen Crohn, Vera Leifman, Dina Rosenfeld, Michelle Benjamin Ruchames, and Paul Ruchames for constant encouragement and general life support. And to my parents, David and Edith Shapiro, who taught me that "if you read a book, you'll never be bored."

And—there is no quote that can do them justice—my feisty, funny, generous, and amazing children, Rachel Brodie, Hayim Daniel Brodie, and Adam Weisberg, to whom this book is lovingly and joyfully dedicated.

Contents

Preface

I have been collecting quotes about writing as long as I have been working with writers—the good, the bad, and the published—for more than twenty-five years. As an editor, I have many opportunities to talk to writers about getting started, juggling writing and real life, overcoming writer's block, finding their voice, revising, and dealing with agents, professional jealousy, fame, and fortune—topics that have become chapters in this book.

The 627 quotes come from sources as diverse as subway posters, *Publishers Weekly*, ballet programs, t-shirts, magazines in my dentist's waiting room, characters in novels, the Bible, handbooks on writing, and newspaper articles. Some were created especially for this book by publishing colleagues, writers I work with, my writing students, and friends. A great many quotes have never appeared in other books.

The people quoted here are not all writers. Other people involved in the arts have a lot to say about the creative process, insights that relate to writing. They represent an extremely broad range: actors, scientists, novelists, dancers, historians, poets, critics, philosophers, and rock stars. Their voices vary from solemn to funny, transcendent to wry. Together they expand our definition of creativity and say more about the process of writing than any single writer could.

Enjoy this book—discover, revisit, and satisfy your desire for the right words when you need them. As the Talmud says, in *Kallah Rabbati*, "A quotation at the right moment is like bread to the hungry." Welcome to the feast!

Definitions of Writers
and Writing

Writing is one-third imagination, one-third experience, and one-
third observation.

—WILLIAM FAULKNER, *novelist*

A novel is gossip trying to pass as art.

—RICHARD PECK, *novelist*

In the novel you get the journey. In a poem you get the arrival.

—MAY SARTON, *poet*

Art is a lie, but lets us see the truth.

—PABLO PICASSO, *painter*

Writing is the process by which you explain to yourself what happened to you.

—ARLENE CROCE, *dance critic*

Any story told twice is fiction.

—GRACE PALEY, *short story writer and poet*

Writing a novel is like driving a car at night. You can only see as far as your headlights, but you can make the whole trip that way.

—E. L. DOCTOROW, *novelist*

I love poetry. It comes so fast. It comes so furiously. Novels take so much preparation and time and planning, but novels allow me to create a whole world.

—NTOZAKE SHANGE, *playwright and poet*

I don't think novels are how-to books. They render experience.

—MARGARET ATWOOD, *novelist and poet*

Southerners do have, they've inherited, a narrative sense of human destiny.

—EUDORA WELTY, *short story writer and novelist*

I create a problem that didn't exist before and solve it to my own satisfaction. That's the creative process.

—AL HIRSCHFELD, *cartoonist*

Creation, whatever its form, is not an act of will, but an act of faith.

—LLOYD ALEXANDER, *novelist*

When you put down the good things you ought to have done, and leave out the bad things you did do, that's memoirs.

—WILL ROGERS, *humorist*

I could no more define poetry than a terrier can a rat, but I thought we both recognized the object by the symptoms which it provokes in us.

—A. E. HOUSMAN, *poet*

I am an eye that sees itself
Look back, a nose that tracks the scent of shadows
As they fall, an ear that picks up sounds
Before they're born. I am the last of the platinum
Retrievers, the end of a gorgeous line.

—MARK STRAND, *poet, "The Greatdog Poems"*

Of the many definitions of poetry, the simplest is still the best: "memorable speech."

—W. H. AUDEN, *poet and essayist*

The poet is not something you become; a poet is something you are.

—JACK PRELUTSKY, *poet*

How to write a poem? Carve a rock you love down to its essence—but keep a weather eye out for crystals of surprise.

—KAY KIDDE, *poet and literary agent*

It is the responsibility of the poet to listen to gossip and pass it on.

—GRACE PALEY, *short story writer and poet*

Poetry is what Milton saw when he went blind.

—DON MARQUIS, *poet and humorist*

A true poet does not bother to be poetical. Nor does a nursery gardener scent his roses.

—JEAN COCTEAU, *dramatist*

Poetry. I like to think of it as statements made on the way to the grave.

—DYLAN THOMAS, *poet*

Poetry today is easier to write but harder to remember.

—STANLEY KUNITZ, *poet*

Poet: Lofty synonym for "blockhead."

—GUSTAVE FLAUBERT, *novelist*

A mystery is a book the publisher thinks will sell better if it has "mystery" on the cover.

—DONALD E. WESTLAKE, *mystery writer*

Biography lends to death a new terror.

—OSCAR WILDE, *dramatist and critic*

Biographies align photographs focused and shot at particular moments in time.

—ROBERT POLITO, *poet and biographer*

An autobiography is an unrivaled vehicle for telling the truth about other people.

—GEORGE LANG, *restaurateur*

Writing an autobiography and making a spiritual will are practically the same.

—SHOLEM ALEICHEM, *novelist and short story writer*

An autobiography must be such that one can sue oneself for libel.

—THOMAS HOVING, *museum director*

Humor is anger that was sent to finishing school.

—RICHARD PECK, *novelist*

Comedy is tragedy plus time.

—CAROL BURNETT, *comedian*

People ask what I am really trying to do with humor. The answer is, "I'm getting even."

—ART BUCHWALD, *humorist*

The creative process of writing is a living amoeba.

—JOAN COLLINS, *actor and novelist*

To be an illustrator is to be a participant. Someone who has something equally important to offer as the writer of the book—occasionally something more important—but is certainly never the writer's echo.

—MAURICE SENDAK, *picture book writer and illustrator*

To write a good love letter, you ought to begin without knowing what you mean to say, and to finish without knowing what you have written.

—JEAN-JACQUES ROUSSEAU, *philosopher*

Translation is like making love through a blanket.

—AMOS OZ, *novelist and essayist*

Translators require the self-effacing disposition of saints.

—ALASTAIR REID, *writer and translator*

Writing about music is like dancing about architecture.

—ELVIS COSTELLO, *songwriter and rock musician*

Melancholy men, they say, are the most incisive humorists; by the same token, writers of fantasy must be, within their own frame of work, hardheaded realists. What appears gossamer is, underneath, solid as prestressed concrete.

—LLOYD ALEXANDER, *novelist*

The correct detail is rarely exactly what happened; the most truthful detail is what *could* have happened, or what *should* have.

—JOHN IRVING, *novelist*

Art makes nothing happen.

—W. H. AUDEN, *poet*

Journalism allows readers to witness history; fiction gives its readers the opportunity to live it.

—JOHN HERSEY, *novelist*

When even one reporter latches on to something, it's like inviting the whole world for tea.

—TAMAR MYERS, *novelist*

Drama has to do with conflict in people, with denials.

—LILLIAN HELLMAN, *playwright*

A screenwriter is a man who is being tortured to confess and has nothing to confess.

—CHRISTOPHER ISHERWOOD, *novelist and playwright*

I don't *ever* write about real people. Art is supposed to be better than that. If you want a slice of life, look out the window.

—BARBARA KINGSOLVER, *novelist*

To think of criticism as a conversation is to think of it as a social act, something that puts you in touch with other people who may think the way you do.

—ARLENE CROCE, *dance critic*

Every writer creates his own precursors.

—JORGE LUIS BORGES, *poet and essayist*

As a writer one of your jobs is to bring news of the world to the world.

—GRACE PALEY, *short story writer and poet*

The artist, like the God of creation, remains within or behind or beyond or above his handiwork, invisible, refined out of existence, indifferent, paring his fingernails.

—JAMES JOYCE, *novelist*

Writing is communication, not self-expression; nobody in this world wants to read your diary, except your mother.

—RICHARD PECK, *novelist*

The Madness of Art

*O*ur doubt is our passion and our passion is our task. The rest is the madness of art.

—HENRY JAMES, *novelist*

The two creatures most to be pitied are the spider and the novelist—their lives hanging by a thread spun out of their own guts.

—KATHERINE PATERSON, *novelist*

Obsession charges all real artists.

—LAR LUBOVITCH, *choreographer*

Writing a book is a long exhausting struggle, like a long bout of some painful illness. One would never undertake such a thing if one were not driven by some demon whom one can neither resist nor understand.

—GEORGE ORWELL, *novelist and essayist*

There is no satisfaction whatever at any time. There is only a queer dissatisfaction; a blessed unrest that keeps us marching and makes us more alive than the others.

—MARTHA GRAHAM, *dancer and choreographer*

The Artistic temperament is a disease that afflicts amateurs.

—G. K. CHESTERTON, *essayist and novelist*

If I can't dance to it, it's not my revolution.

—EMMA GOLDMAN, *political activist*

I've found that talent and humility are not first cousins.

—MEG O'BRIEN, *radio show host*

It is important not to be too confident. In fact, in my opinion, it is good to be constantly scared. Fear can be healthy if it does not cripple you.

—LUCIANO PAVAROTTI, *opera singer*

It's very important, I think, to keep yourself on a level of absolute uncertainty as to whether you can do anything.

—MARTIN SCORSESE, *film director*

Any book is a casting of runes, a reading of cards, a map of the palm and heart. We make up the ocean—then fall in. But we also write the life raft.

—ERICA JONG, *poet and novelist*

When my writing is going well, I know that I'm writing out of my personal obsessions.

—BHARATI MUKHERJEE, *novelist*

Poetry—excites us to artificial feelings—callous to real ones.

—SAMUEL TAYLOR COLERIDGE, *poet*

A good writer sells out everybody he knows, sooner or later.

—ALICE MCDERMOTT, *novelist*

If a writer has to rob his mother, he will not hesitate; the "Ode on a Grecian Urn" is worth any number of old ladies.

—WILLIAM FAULKNER, *novelist*

I attack the stone with violence. Is this to tame it or to awaken myself?

—ISAMU NOGUCHI, *sculptor*

Writers do tend to devour people, themselves included.

—ERICA JONG, *poet and novelist*

You don't have to suffer to be a poet. Adolescence is enough suffering for anyone.

—JOHN CIARDI, *poet and essayist*

It is not that you have to be happy—that would be asking too much—but if it gets too painful that sense of wonderment, or joy, dies, and with it the generosity so necessary to create.

—EDNA O'BRIEN, *novelist and short story writer*

It is impossible to experience one's own death objectively and still carry a tune.

—WOODY ALLEN, *filmmaker and humorist*

What Makes a Good Story?

*T*here are three rules to writing the novel. Unfortunately, no one
knows what they are.

—W. SOMERSET MAUGHAM, *novelist*

Cut a good story anywhere, and it will bleed.

—ANTON CHEKHOV, *dramatist and short story writer*

Vigorous writing is concise. This requires not that the writer make all
his sentences short, or that he avoid all detail, but that every word tell.

—WILLIAM STRUNK, *professor of English*

Just keep the thing going any way you can.

—TENNESSEE WILLIAMS, *playwright*

It is always better to give a little less than the reader wants, than more.

—MAXWELL PERKINS, *editor*

When people say that less is more, I say *more* is more. *Less* is *less.* I go
for more.

—DOLLY PARTON, *singer and songwriter*

Too much of a good thing can be wonderful.

—MAE WEST, *actor and screenwriter*

Always grab the reader by the throat in the first paragraph, sink your
thumbs into his windpipe in the second, and hold him against the wall
until the tag line.

—PAUL O'NEIL, *marketer*

Fashion passes, style remains.

—COCO CHANEL, *fashion designer*

Style and structure are the essence of a good book; great ideas
are hogwash.

—VLADIMIR NABOKOV, *novelist*

If you get the form of things right, every peril can be tamed.

—DICK FRANCIS, *novelist*

A square dish without corners, what sort of square dish is that?

—CONFUCIUS, *philosopher*

Even in nice Mr. Stevenson's stories, each boy's life only catches
your deepest interest when a pirate is about to slit that sweet
child's throat. What makes a story good ain't what makes a person good.
Why is that?

—ALLAN GURGANUS, *novelist*

What is the use of a book without pictures or conversations?

—LEWIS CARROLL, *novelist and mathematician*

Nothing much happens in Jane Austen's books, and yet, when you come
to the bottom of the page, you eagerly turn it to learn what will happen
next. Nothing very much does and again you eagerly turn the page. The
novelist who has the power to achieve this has the most precious gift a
novelist can possess.

—W. SOMERSET MAUGHAM, *novelist*

Only the rarest kind of best in anything can be good enough for
the young.

—WALTER DE LA MARE, *poet*

I am going to give them crime and blood and three murders a chapter; such is the insanity of the age that I do not doubt for one moment the success of the venture.

—EDGAR WALLACE, *novelist*

There's an old adage in writing: "Don't tell, but show." . . . Writing is not psychology. We do not talk "about" feelings. Instead the writer feels and through her words awakens those feelings in the reader. The writer takes the reader's hand and guides him through the valley of sorrow and joy without ever having to mention those words.

—NATALIE GOLDBERG, *poet and writing teacher*

My grandfather was lame. Once they asked him to tell a story about his teacher. And he related how the holy Baal Shem used to hop and dance while he prayed. My grandfather rose as he spoke, and he was so swept away by his story that he himself began to hop and dance to show how the master had done. From that hour on he was cured of his lameness. That's the way to tell a story!

—MARTIN BUBER, *philosopher*

Preaching is fatal to art in literature.

—STEPHEN CRANE, *novelist*

To write simply is as difficult as to be good.

—W. SOMERSET MAUGHAM, *novelist*

I wasn't, and am not *primarily* concerned with injustice, but with art.

—RALPH ELLISON, *novelist and essayist*

In comedy, morality matters less than vitality.

—JOHN POWERS, *movie critic*

Pithy sentences are like sharp nails which force truth upon our memory.

—DENIS DIDEROT, *philosopher and encyclopedist*

Make everything as simple as possible, but not simpler.

—ALBERT EINSTEIN, *scientist and philosopher*

A book that furnishes no quotation is, *me judice,* no book—it is
a plaything.

—THOMAS LOVE PEACOCK, *novelist*

First have something to say, second say it, third stop when you have said
it, and finally give it an accurate title.

—JOHN SHAW BILLINGS, *nonfiction writer*

A good poem . . . wouldn't try to give comfort or fun to people: it
would be good because of what it was, not because of what it did.

—LAURA RIDING, *poet*

A novel can educate to some extent. But first, a novel has to entertain—that's the contract with the reader: you give me ten hours and I'll give you a reason to turn every page.

—BARBARA KINGSOLVER, *novelist*

No tears in the writer, no tears in the reader. No surprise for the writer, no surprise for the reader.

—ROBERT FROST, *poet*

In a lot of books I read, the writer seems to go haywire every time he reaches a high point. He'll start leaving out punctuation and running his words together and babble about stars flashing and sinking into a deep dreamless sea. And you can't figure out whether the hero's laying his girl or a cornerstone.

—JIM THOMPSON, *novelist*

You can do anything you can get away with, but nobody has ever gotten away with much.

—FLANNERY O'CONNOR, *novelist and short story writer*

I try to leave out the parts that people skip.

—ELMORE LEONARD, *novelist*

Getting Started

*Y*ou just sit down and write every day for three or four hours. You do it like piano scales until you have a story to tell.

—ANNE LAMOTT, *novelist and essayist*

Convince yourself that you are working in clay not marble, on paper not eternal bronze: let that first sentence be as stupid as it wishes. No one will rush out and print it as it stands. Just put it down; then another.

—JACQUES BARZUN, *historian and essayist*

The only joy in the world is to begin.

—CESARE PAVESE, *novelist and poet*

It may be better if you don't know *what* before you begin. You ought to be able to discover something from your stories. If you don't, probably nobody else will.

—FLANNERY O'CONNOR, *novelist and short story writer*

The only reason to write a first novel is if you absolutely cannot *not*.

—CLAIRE M. SMITH, *literary agent*

Get a grasp on your subject and the words will follow.

—CATO THE ELDER, *Roman statesman and writer*

Too often I wait for the sentence to finish taking shape in my mind before setting it down. It is better to seize it by the end that first offers itself, head or foot, though not knowing the rest, then pull: the rest will follow along.

—ANDRÉ GIDE, *novelist*

You don't decide to write a poem, the poem decides that you will write it.

—GAD YAACOBI, *poet and diplomat*

Images always come first.

—C. S. Lewis, *novelist and essayist*

I took a clean white piece of paper—like a sheet freshly ironed for making love—and rolled it into the carriage. I wrote my name, and immediately the words began to flow, one thing linked to another and another. Characters stepped from the shadows, each with a face, a voice, passions, and obsessions.

—Isabel Allende, *novelist*

It is a journey into the unknown where often you're only conscious of, and what's only visible for you is, that step right in front of you. But you take it and you hope. And when you look up you've reached San Francisco.

—Gloria Naylor, *novelist*

Travel fixes something that has always been out of kilter—and lets the writing begin.

—FRANCINE PROSE, *novelist*

Acrobats start their children on the high wire as soon as they can walk, and a writer ought to begin before he has graduated to solid food.

—ROBERTSON DAVIES, *novelist and essayist*

I start my work by asking a question and then try to answer it.

—MARY LEE SETTLE, *novelist*

Just sit down at the typewriter and open a vein.

—RED SMITH, *sportswriter*

Reading Trash and Classics

*B*eing a writer in a library is rather like being a eunuch in a harem.

—JOHN BRAINE, *novelist*

Read, read, read. Read everything—trash, classics, good and bad, and see how they do it. Read! You'll absorb it. Then write. If it is good, you'll find out. If it's not, throw it out the window.

—WILLIAM FAULKNER, *novelist*

Be sure that you go to the author to get at *his* meaning, not to find yours.

—JOHN RUSKIN, *critic and essayist*

That I can read and be happy while I am reading, is a great blessing.

—ANTHONY TROLLOPE, *novelist*

An ingrained ear for language comes from reading good literature and balances the domestic babble, street talk, advertising drivel, and work jargon ravaging our brains.

—ARTHUR PLOTNIK, *editor*

I never can get interested in things that didn't happen to people who never lived.

—HELENE HANFF, *scriptwriter and journalist*

When you read a classic you do not see in the book more than you did before. You see in you more than there was before.

—CLIFTON FADIMAN, *critic*

One always tends to overpraise a long book because one has got through it.

—E. M. FORSTER, *novelist*

Professors of literature collect books the way a ship collects barnacles, without seeming effort. A literary academic can no more pass a bookstore than an alcoholic can pass a bar.

—AMANDA CROSS, *novelist*

When a new book is published, read an old one.

—SAMUEL ROGERS, *poet*

My best friend is a person who will give me a book I have not read.

—ABRAHAM LINCOLN, *U.S. president*

Read the greatest stuff but read the stuff that isn't so great, too. Great stuff is very discouraging. If you read only Beckett and Chekhov, you'll go away and only deliver telegrams at Western Union.

—EDWARD ALBEE, *playwright*

People without hope not only don't write novels, but what is more to the point, they don't read them. The way to despair is to refuse to have any kind of experience, and the novel, of course, is a way to have experience.

—FLANNERY O'CONNOR, *novelist and short story writer*

When we read, we start at the beginning and continue until we reach the end; when we write, we start in the middle and fight our way out.

—VICKIE KARP, *poet*

It is odd enough that my own individual taste is for quite another class of works than those which I myself am able to write. If I were to meet with such books as mine by another writer, I don't believe I should be able to get through them.

—NATHANIEL HAWTHORNE, *novelist*

I never read any novels except my own.

—BARBARA CARTLAND, *novelist*

Libraries shelter students and give the impression that strong fires burn in adjoining rooms.

—MARK HELPRIN, *novelist and speechwriter*

A book must be the ax for the frozen sea within us.

—FRANZ KAFKA, *novelist and short story writer*

We read to know we're not alone.

—C. S. LEWIS, *novelist and essayist*

When we are collecting books, we are collecting happiness.

—VINCENT STARRETT, *novelist*

Teaching and Mentoring

$\mathcal{T}$eaching is a superb way of training yourself to be a better reader, which is what you have to do to be a better writer anyway.

—JIM SHEPARD, *novelist*

If you want to be a writer, don't listen to any advice given by writers.

—JON SCIESZKA, *picture book writer*

I made a choice to work in the university in order to preserve a kind of nonchalance with regard to publication.

—SEAMUS HEANEY, *poet*

Who will teach me what I must shun? Or must I go where the impulse drives?

—JOHANN WOLFGANG VON GOETHE, *poet*

Directors, coaches, and editors cannot teach you how to get there. But they can put you on the paths that *lead* there.

—THOMAS MCCORMACK, *editor and publisher*

This is what I can "teach" a young writer: something he'll know for himself in a little while longer; but why wait to know these things? I am talking about technical things, the only things you can presume to teach, anyway.

—JOHN IRVING, *novelist*

If I say that [novelist] Henry Green taught me how to write it implies that I learned, and it is not a business one learns—unlearns rather.

—JOHN UPDIKE, *novelist and short story writer*

We want competence, but competence itself is deadly. What you want is the vision to go with it, and you do not get this from a writing class.

—FLANNERY O'CONNOR, *novelist and short story writer*

Maybe writing can't be taught, but editing *can* be taught—prayer, fasting, and self-mutilation.

—DONALD BARTHELME, *novelist and short story writer*

All I am doing is pointing. You must find it true for yourself.

—THE BUDDHA

Time is a great teacher.

—CARL SANDBURG, *poet*

When the student is ready, the teacher will appear.

—CHINESE PROVERB

Inspiration

A poet is someone who stands outside in the rain hoping to get struck by lightning.

—JAMES DICKEY, *poet and novelist*

You can't wait for inspiration. You have to go after it with a club.

—JACK LONDON, *novelist*

A poem begins with poetry, not with an idea for poetry.

—P. D. JAMES, *novelist*

True ease in writing comes from art, not chance,
As those move easiest who have learned to dance.

—ALEXANDER POPE, *poet, "An Essay on Criticism"*

Creativity is more like a slot machine than a vending machine.

—MARSHALL J. COOK, *writing teacher*

Imagination is more important than knowledge.

—ALBERT EINSTEIN, *scientist and philosopher*

If I had to live my life again, I would make a rule to read some poetry
and listen to some music at least once a week; for perhaps the parts of
my brain now atrophied would thus have been kept active through use.

—CHARLES DARWIN, *scientist*

It's amazing the things people will tell you, especially when one is a
writer. I feel I'm constantly swimming through this maze of stories.

—JOHN GUARE, *playwright*

Inspiration is to work every day.

—CHARLES BAUDELAIRE, *poet*

Know something, sugar? Stories only happen to the people who can
tell them.

—ALLAN GURGANUS, *novelist*

A deadline is negative inspiration. Still, it's better than no inspiration at all.

—RITA MAE BROWN, *novelist*

It is not every day that the world arranges itself into a poem.

—WALLACE STEVENS, *poet*

I feel it in me like a woman having a baby, all that life churning on inside me. I feel it every day: it moves, stretches, yawns. It's getting ready to get born. It knows exactly what it is.

—MAURICE SENDAK, *picture book writer and illustrator*

The more I yearned, the more I wrote. Yearning is an essential emotion for a poet.

—ERICA JONG, *poet and novelist*

You do not need to leave your room. Remain sitting at your table and listen. Do not even listen, simply wait, be quite still and solitary. The world will freely offer itself to you to be unmasked, it has no choice, it will roll in ecstasy at your feet.

—FRANZ KAFKA, *novelist and short story writer*

If you have to urge a writing student to "gain experience with life," he is probably never going to be a writer. Any life will provide the material for writing, if it is attended to.

—WALLACE STEGNER, *novelist*

Inspiration usually comes during work, rather than before it.

—MADELEINE L'ENGLE, *novelist*

To work with limitations frees intuition.

—CHUCK CLOSE, *painter*

If you're silent for a long time, people just arrive in your mind.

—ALICE WALKER, *novelist and poet*

The muse in charge of fantasy wears good, sensible shoes. No foam-born Aphrodite, she vaguely resembles my old piano teacher, who was keen on metronomes. She does not carry a soothing lyre for inspiration, but is more likely to shake you roughly awake at four in the morning and rattle a sheaf of subtle, sneaky questions under your nose. And you had better answer them. Her geometries are no more Euclidian than Einstein's, but they are equally rigorous.

—LLOYD ALEXANDER, *novelist*

I see the notion of talent as quite irrelevant. I see instead perseverance, application, industry, assiduity, will, will, will, desire, desire, desire.

—GORDON LISH, *editor and writing teacher*

In dreams begin responsibilities.

—DELMORE SCHWARTZ, *poet and short story writer*

There's always something new by looking at the same thing over and over.

—JOHN UPDIKE, *novelist and short story writer*

As a writer, all I need is peacefulness and postage.

—CYNTHIA RYLANT, *novelist*

Writer's Block

You don't know what it is to stay a whole day with your head
in your hands trying to squeeze your unfortunate brain so as to
find a word.

—GUSTAVE FLAUBERT, *novelist*

Writer's block is a temporary paralysis caused by the
conviction, on an unconscious level, that what the writer is attempting is
in some way fraudulent, or mistaken, or self-destructive.

—JOYCE CAROL OATES, *novelist*

The impulse to keep to yourself what you have learned is not only shameful, it is destructive. Anything you do not give freely and abundantly becomes lost to you. You open your safe and find ashes.

—ANNIE DILLARD, *naturalist and essayist*

Any productive writer learns that you can't wait for inspiration. That's a recipe for writer's block.

—SUSAN SONTAG, *essayist*

People who can't afford to have writer's block don't get it. That tells you everything you need to know about writer's block.

—MARSHALL J. COOK, *writing teacher*

The perfect pointed pencil—the paper persuasive—the fantastic chair and a good light and no writing.

—JOHN STEINBECK, *novelist*

You have to allow yourself the liberty of writing poorly. You have to get the bulk of it done, and then you start to refine it. You have to put down less than marvelous material just to keep going to whatever you think the end is going to be—which may be something else altogether by the time you get there.

—LARRY GELBART, *scriptwriter*

I've never had a day where I couldn't write 15 pages. Some days, it's horrible, some days I don't know what language it's in. But I know I'll go back and fix it up.

—R. L. STINE, *novelist*

Writer's block is far more frequently found in the presence of too much, not too little, will. Creative discipline grows out of pleasure, not out of tyranny or self-abuse.

—VICTORIA NELSON, *essayist and short story writer*

It doesn't get easier. What appears to be "ease" may be mainly will-power struggling against entropy.

—SUZANNE NEWTON, *novelist*

I have forced myself to begin writing when I've been utterly exhausted, when I've felt my soul as thin as a playing card . . . and somehow the activity of writing changes everything.

—JOYCE CAROL OATES, *novelist*

Work Habits

Write a verse a day, not to send to publishers, but to throw in waste baskets. It will help your prose. It will give you swing.

—DR. SEUSS, *author and illustrator*

When you are not writing, you are a writer too. It doesn't leave you. Walk with an animal walk and take in everything around you as prey.

—NATALIE GOLDBERG, *poet and writing teacher*

Most writing is done away from the typewriter, away from the desk. I'd say it occurs in the quiet, silent moments, while you're walking or playing a game, or even talking to someone you're not vitally interested in. You're working, your mind is working, on this problem in the back of your head.

—HENRY MILLER, *novelist*

I tend to work on a group of things so that one of them will speak to me in some way and need something, rather than to try to sit in front of the work until I can get an idea for it.

—ROY LICHTENSTEIN, *painter*

I know a good many fiction writers who paint, not because they're any good at painting, but because it helps their writing. It forces them to look at things.

—FLANNERY O'CONNOR, *novelist and short story writer*

Break off work when you "are going good." Then you can rest easily and on the next day easily resume.

—ERNEST HEMINGWAY, *novelist and short story writer*

It helps if you have someone to talk to, it really helps. I don't think you can write a book completely alone.

—JUDITH KRANTZ, *novelist*

Fiction was like pie-crust dough. After working it you had to let it cool.

—RICHARD HALL, *novelist*

When I'm working on a first draft, sometimes I actually delete an entire chapter from the [computer] memory so I have to type it all over, because that's the only way I can relive it. I have to stay close to these people, I have to have their experiences, too, and the only way to do that is to start all over. It can be very exciting, and it can be very painful, but I have to make the emotional investment.

—TERRY McMILLAN, *novelist*

I write fast, because I have not the brains to write slow.

—GEORGES SIMENON, *novelist*

I wouldn't dream of trying out my ideas on children or anyone else. A book should be the work of an author's imagination—not the work of a committee.

—BEVERLY CLEARY, *novelist*

I don't take all that many notes, and sometimes it's largely to keep myself awake. And I never refer to them later. The more fun I have, the fewer notes I take. I don't write the review [during the performance]. That's fatal.

—ARLENE CROCE, *dance critic*

When my editor asked me to discard my outline and synopsis, what a
relief it was! Before, I felt as if I had already written the book. But now
I go to my word processor every morning, eager to find out what
happens next.

—MARY JANE MILLER, *novelist*

I never write exercises, but sometimes I write poems which fail and call
them exercises.

—ROBERT FROST, *poet*

I usually get the title for a book first, and I type it up immediately. I sit
there and look at it and admire it, and I think to myself, I just need
four thousand sentences to go with this and I'll have a book. It is such
a pleasurable moment that I type many more title pages than I could
ever use.

—BETSY BYARS, *novelist*

The faster I write the better my output. If I'm going slow I'm in
trouble. It means I'm pushing the words instead of being pulled
by them.

—RAYMOND CHANDLER, *novelist*

This diary writing has greatly helped my style; loosened the ligatures.

—VIRGINIA WOOLF, *novelist*

If you can't find your inspiration by walking around the block one time, go around two blocks—but never three.

—ROBERT MOTHERWELL, *painter*

When I am ready to write a book, I write the ending first.

—MARCIA DAVENPORT, *novelist*

I think it hurts a writer to have his secrets known—his method of working disclosed while he is still active. It would bother me; so much of writing is a fragile thing, so much depends on one's ability to maintain illusion. I don't want the privacy of that invaded in any way.

—BERNARD MALAMUD, *novelist*

Juggling Writing and Real Life

I was writing—learning and growing along with the children—until eventually I was writing fiction worthy of publication. It might have happened sooner had I had a room of my own and fewer children, but somehow I doubt it. For as I look back on what I have written, I can see that the very persons who have taken away my time and space are those who have given me something to say.

—KATHERINE PATERSON, *novelist*

Growing up with five brothers taught me that it's good to be the guy telling the story after the lamp gets broken.

—JON SCIESZKA, *picture book writer*

If it happens to you, use it. Hear it, feel it, refine it, use it.

—PAULA DANZIGER, *novelist*

You must always plant your feet firmly on the ground if you want to be able to jump up in the air.

—JOAN MIRÓ, *painter*

The world was something that a poet had to roll around in, personally becoming a sort of breaded veal cutlet of the spirit.

—ALLAN GURGANUS, *novelist*

Life and art were too close, like *Titanic* and iceberg.

—D. M. THOMAS, *novelist*

To be happy, you must have something fulfilling in your life that has nothing to do with your work, because there's a terrible tendency to wait for the phone to ring. I want my life to feed the work. I don't want it to be something that happens only between jobs.

—BARBARA HERSHEY, *actor*

You have to pace yourself. Life is a marathon, not a sprint.

—MARY LANDRIEU, *U.S. Senator from Louisiana*

When I'm working, I can't distance myself. I can't stop to make a pot roast when I'm holding everything in my mind. My children learned to amuse themselves at times like that. They always knew it wouldn't take that long if they left me alone. They knew I meant business.

—MERRILL JOAN GERBER, *novelist*

If you want to lose weight, don't do it while you're working on a major project.

—RITA MAE BROWN, *novelist*

Two hours of writing fiction leaves this particular writer absolutely drained. For those two hours he has been miles away, he has been somewhere else, in a different place with totally different people, and the effort of swimming back into normal surroundings is very great.

—ROALD DAHL, *novelist*

I'm sometimes afraid I'll cross a line and it'll be difficult to come back, say, to dinner.

—JAMAICA KINCAID, *novelist*

Composition seems to me impossible with a head full of joints of mutton and doses of rhubarb.

—JANE AUSTEN, *novelist*

If you want to be a writer, somewhere along the line you're going to have to hurt somebody. And when that time comes, you go ahead and do it.

—CHARLES MCGRATH, *editor*

I love being a writer. What I hate is the paperwork.

—PETER DEVRIES, *novelist*

How important it is to take the time to read literature, to look at art, to go to concerts. If all parts of your brain aren't nourished, you become really limited—less sensitive. It's like food. You'd get pretty strange if you ate ice cream all the time.

—KENT NAGANO, *orchestra conductor*

Nothing can interest the creator but his own work.

—MARCEL PROUST, *novelist*

It is not often that someone comes along who is a true friend and a good writer.

—E. B. WHITE, *novelist and essayist*

The writer is not the person, yet both natures are true.

—FAY WELDON, *novelist*

If no one notices it, don't do it. If you have to dust, water, polish or feed it, you don't need it. Don't clean your house, strip it.

—ELAINE FANTLE SHIMBERG, *nonfiction writer*

In order to be an artist, one must be deeply rooted in the society.

—SIMONE DE BEAUVOIR, *novelist and essayist*

He is a man of thirty-five, but looks fifty. He is bald, has varicose veins and wears spectacles, or would wear them if his only pair were not chronically lost. If things are normal with him, he will be suffering from malnutrition, but if he has recently had a lucky streak, he will be suffering from a hangover. At present it is half past eleven in the morning, and according to his schedule he should have started work two hours ago; but even if he had made any serious effort to start he would have been frustrated by the almost continuous ringing of the telephone bell, the yells of the baby, the rattle of an electric drill out in the street, and the heavy boots of his creditors clumping up the stairs. . . .
Needless to say this person is a writer.

—GEORGE ORWELL, *novelist and essayist*

Books, if you don't put them first, tend to sulk. They retreat into a corner and refuse to work.

—SALMAN RUSHDIE, *novelist*

All you need is a room without any particular interruptions.

—JOHN DOS PASSOS, *novelist*

A sudden beam of moonlight, a girl you've just kissed, or a beautiful view through your study window is seldom the source of an urge to put words on paper. Such pleasant experiences are more likely to delay one's work.

—OSCAR HAMMERSTEIN II, *lyricist*

I experienced writer enlightenment as I was writing kids' mid-year progress reports. I realized that I couldn't write one more "Jennifer needs to take more risks to become a better learner" until I did what I was asking them to do. I took off the next year of teaching to write.

—JON SCIESZKA, *picture book writer*

The goal is paramount. One's mate is present, therefore, as an effective and useful aide-de-camp or as an impediment. Guilt is the one overload [the novelist] will not accept. He cannot afford it.

—NORMAN MAILER, *novelist*

One cannot think well if one has not dined well.

—VIRGINIA WOOLF, *novelist*

Sex, Drugs, and Rock 'n' Roll

*B*e regular and orderly in your life, so that you may be violent and
original in your work.

—GUSTAVE FLAUBERT, *novelist*

People doubt that I'm a writer when I tell them I don't drink much:
writers are supposed to pass their life apprenticeships in saloons.

—PHILIP LOPATE, *essayist and novelist*

An alcoholic is someone you don't like who drinks as much as you do.

—DYLAN THOMAS, *poet*

I realize that I am much too clean to be a genius, much too sober to be a champ, and far, far too clumsy with a shotgun to live the good life.

—RAYMOND CHANDLER, *novelist*

I used to drink occasionally and take a little grass now and again back when I was real young. And I thought that I could write an awful lot better if I did. But it wasn't very good. It seemed wonderful at the time. Marvelous. I'd look at it the next day and say, "What the hell was that all about?"

—EDWARD ALBEE, *playwright*

You see, baby, after a glass or two of wine I'm inclined to extravagance. I'm inclined to excesses because I drink while I'm writing, so I'll blue pencil a lot the next day.

—TENNESSEE WILLIAMS, *playwright*

It's difficult to write well about sex. It is so easy to lapse into parody since it's such a charged area of our experience. And one for which we have a very crude and awkward vocabulary because of the taboo surrounding the subject. It is very difficult to write subtly in a way that doesn't induce inadvertent mirth.

—JAY MCINERNEY, *novelist*

I've led a good rich sexual life, and I don't see why it should be left out.

—HENRY MILLER, *novelist*

All a writer has to do to get a woman is to say he's a writer. It's an aphrodisiac.

—SAUL BELLOW, *novelist*

Change the name of the hero of the story and you've got a record of my licentious life. So why do I need biographers?

—ISAAC BASHEVIS SINGER, *novelist*

My stories written when sober are stupid.

—F. SCOTT FITZGERALD, *novelist*

Some American writers who have known each other for years have never met in the daytime or when both were sober.

—JAMES THURBER, *humorist*

One of the reasons why many writers turn into alcoholics is that early in their lives they find that getting drunk is part of the creative process, that it opens up visions. It's a terrible sort of creative device, because three out of four who involve themselves in it become alcoholics. But it does open up doors in the beginning.

—MALCOLM COWLEY, *essayist and critic*

Drunks ramble; so do books by drunks.

—JOHN IRVING, *novelist*

I think booze is wonderful. The problem is that the window of creativity becomes smaller and smaller. You sit down, have a drink, smoke a cigarette, have another drink and the blank page is still blank.

—PETE TOWNSHEND, *songwriter and guitarist*

Reality is a crutch for people who can't cope with drugs.

—LILY TOMLIN, *comedian*

Subject and Plot

A story is: The king died, the queen died. A plot is: The king died, the queen died of grief.

—E. M. FORSTER, *novelist*

There are only two or three human stories, and they go on repeating themselves as fiercely as if they had never happened before.

—WILLA CATHER, *novelist*

You divert [the reader], then you clobber him.

—FLANNERY O'CONNOR, *novelist and short story writer*

When I used to teach creative writing, I would tell students to make their characters want something right away even if it's only a glass of water. Characters paralyzed by the meaninglessness of modern life still have to drink water from time to time.

—KURT VONNEGUT, *novelist*

Plots are just one thing after another, a what and a what and a what.

—MARGARET ATWOOD, *novelist and poet*

I believe in plot. I want an English professor to understand the symbolism while at the same time I want the people I grew up with—who may not often read anything but the Sears catalogue—to read my books.

—BARBARA KINGSOLVER, *novelist*

Real suspense comes with moral dilemma and the courage to make and act upon choices. False suspense comes from the accidental and meaningless occurrence of one damned thing after another.

—JOHN GARDNER, *novelist and writing teacher*

Writing about writing, Chekhov instructs us that no gun should go off unless we have first shown it hanging on the wall: every surprise must have its sublimated genesis.

—CYNTHIA OZICK, *novelist*

Hindsight can give structure to anything, but you have to be able to see it.

—CAROL SHIELDS, *novelist*

Get your character in trouble in the first sentence and out of trouble in the last sentence.

—BARTHE DECLEMENTS, *novelist*

There are thirty-two ways to write a story, and I've used every one, but there is only one plot—things are not as they seem.

—JIM THOMPSON, *novelist*

The writer, like the murderer, needs a motive.

—JANET MALCOLM, *journalist*

A novel is a question, not an answer.

—RICHARD PECK, *novelist*

Technique is only a telephone wire—what's important is the message going through it.

—KENT NAGANO, *orchestra conductor*

Years ago someone said to me, "Jackson, your books must be printed on scar tissue." I was pleased.

—RICHARD JACKSON, *editor and publisher*

The problem with evil is one of the central preoccupations of literature. As novelists, we're more drawn to exploring the dark side of human nature than the light side. We'll never be out of work.

—JAY MCINERNEY, *novelist*

The heart of darkness is in our own backyard.

—PHILIP CAPUTO, *novelist and memoirist*

Say it, say it. The universe is made of stories, not of atoms.

—MURIEL RUKEYSER, *poet*

There is no greater cruelty than banality. How dare my parents not give me anything to write about!

—POLLY FROST, *playwright and reviewer*

When the plot flags, bring in a man with a gun.

—RAYMOND CHANDLER, *novelist*

Fiction, Nonfiction, and Genre

*E*ach time I *agree* with myself, I write an essay. When I *disagree* with myself, I know that I'm pregnant with a short story or a novel.

—AMOS OZ, *novelist and essayist*

The overwhelming problem that I see with most biographies and histories is that there's no theme: they're stories, and they need to be about something.

—RON CHERNOW, *historian and biographer*

Readers of biographies like their meat rare.

—ROBERTSON DAVIES, *novelist*

A biographer and his subject become locked in a contest of
undetermined duration, over issues that are always in dispute, for stakes
that are never clearly delineated. It's like a marriage.

—RONALD STEEL, *biographer*

Everything that makes you a good nonfiction writer gets in the way of
the first draft of fiction. I'm just flabbergasted at what my unconscious
mind knows that my conscious mind doesn't know. It's what you have to
tap with fiction, and it's scary.

—SOPHY BURNHAM, *novelist and nonfiction writer*

Fiction is not photography, it's oil painting.

—ROBERTSON DAVIES, *novelist*

One thing about writing biography is that you tend to focus less on
your own life.

—CAROL SHIELDS, *novelist*

The nice thing about a play is you can luxuriate in dialogue, in a way
you can't in movies. My concern in movies is to keep it moving.

—ANDREW BERGMAN, *screenwriter and director*

Writing for children is not easier, it's not nicer, not different from "real" writing; it's the same thing.

—MARGARET GABEL, *writing teacher*

In a mystery, you must play fair by giving all the clues, but disguise them by immediately distracting the reader with something else.

—JOAN LOWERY NIXON, *novelist*

Farce needs desperation. It needs people with different agendas being trapped in a room together.

—SCOTT RUDIN, *Hollywood producer*

The task of the nonfiction writer is to find the story—the narrative line—that exists in nearly every subject, be it the life of a person or the life of a cell.

—RUSSELL FREEDMAN, *nonfiction writer*

Voice and Style

I found I was repeating myself. It is the beginning of the end when you discover you have style.

—DASHIELL HAMMETT, *novelist*

The difference between the right word and the almost right word is the difference between lightning and lightning-bug.

—MARK TWAIN, *humorist*

Some people worry that slang will somehow "corrupt" the language. We should be so lucky.

—STEVEN PINKER, *novelist*

Content without style is propaganda or adolescence. Style without content is decadence.

—RITA MAE BROWN, *novelist*

Prose is architecture, not decoration.

—ERNEST HEMINGWAY, *novelist and short story writer*

A novelist's vice usually resembles his virtue, for what he does best he also tends to do to excess.

—JOHN IRVING, *novelist*

Maybe we're here only to say: house, bridge, well, gate, jug, olive-tree, window—at most, pillar, tower—but to say them, remember, oh! to say them in a way that the things themselves never dreamed of so intensely.

—RAINER MARIA RILKE, *poet*

The little bit (two inches wide) of ivory on which I work with so fine a brush as produces little effect after much labor.

—JANE AUSTEN, *novelist*

There are voices that stand out, like the voice at the dinner table whose next sentence you strain to hear.

—LOUISE GLÜCK, *poet*

Don't say it was "delightful"; make *us* say "delightful" when we've read the description. You see, all those words (horrifying, wonderful, hideous, exquisite) are only like saying to your readers "Please will you do my job for me."

—C. S. LEWIS, *novelist*

A simile must be as precise as a slide rule and as natural as the smell of dill.

—ISAAC BABEL, *novelist*

You do not create a style. You work, and develop yourself; your style is an emanation from your own being.

—KATHERINE ANNE PORTER, *novelist*

Words are like bodies and meanings are like souls, and the body is like a vessel for the soul.

—ABRAHAM IBN EZRA, *poet and philosopher*

Don't use words too big for the subject. Don't say "infinitely" when you mean "very"; otherwise you'll have no word left when you want to talk about something *really* infinite.

—C. S. LEWIS, *novelist*

The difficulty of literature is not to write, but to write what you mean; not to affect your reader, but to affect him precisely as you wish.

—ROBERT LOUIS STEVENSON, *novelist and poet*

Words are all we have.

—SAMUEL BECKETT, *playwright*

The English language has a deceptive air of simplicity; so have some little frocks; but they are both not the kind that any fool can run up in half an hour with a machine.

—DOROTHY L. SAYERS, *novelist*

My object as a writer is to disappear into the voice of a story, to *become* that voice.

—MICHAEL DORRIS, *novelist*

Sometimes after a day of writing I have gone to a party and been refreshed by the fact that I didn't have to make up any of the dialogue I was hearing, or write it down, or take any trouble with it at all. Although sometimes I have thought some of the dialogue could be improved.

—MICHAEL CADNUM, *poet and novelist*

Give me the right word and the right accent and I will move the
world.

—JOSEPH CONRAD, *novelist*

To produce the truly singable thing, that's a glory, isn't it?

—THEODORE ROETHKE, *poet*

Characters

A human being is nothing but a story with skin around it.

—FRED ALLEN, *humorist*

Plot springs from character. . . . I've always sort of believed
that these people inside of me—these characters—know who
they are and what they're about and what happens, and they
need me to help get it down on paper because they
don't type.

—ANNE LAMOTT, *novelist and essayist*

To Guildenstern and Rosencrantz, Hamlet was a minor player.

—HENRY MILLER, *novelist*

Characters are fascinating in their extremity not in their happiness.

—ELIZABETH GEORGE, *novelist*

Find out what your hero or heroine wants, and when he or she wakes up
in the morning, just follow him or her all day.

—RAY BRADBURY, *novelist and short story writer*

The poor novelist constructs his characters; he controls them and makes
them speak. The true novelist listens to them and watches them
function; he eavesdrops on them even before he knows them.

—ANDRÉ GIDE, *novelist*

Always write the characters you disagree with stronger than the ones you
agree with.

—JONATHAN TOLIN, *novelist*

Characters accrete. They are composites. Who knows where they come
from? You hear a phrase, you notice a look, all sorts of impressions
come to you.

—NADINE GORDIMER, *novelist*

Don't write about Man, write about a man.

—E. B. White, *essayist and novelist*

It may be possible in novel-writing to present characters successfully
without telling a story: but it is not possible to tell a story successfully
without presenting characters.

—Wilkie Collins, *novelist*

Nothing is as important as a likable narrator. Nothing holds a story
together better.

—Ethan Canin, *novelist*

The women who came West were as strong as the men. I treat women
with respect in my stories.

—Louis L'Amour, *Western novelist*

Begin with an individual, and before you know it you find that you have
created a type. Begin with a type and you find that you have created—
nothing.

—F. Scott Fitzgerald, *novelist*

I give them their heads. They furnish their own nooses.

—Dawn Powell, *novelist*

[The novelist's] characters, the creations of his brain, must be with him as he lies down to sleep, and as he wakes from his dreams. He must learn to hate them and to love them. He must argue with them, quarrel with them, forgive them, and even submit to them.

—ANTHONY TROLLOPE, *novelist*

These characters in my mind are not real. They aren't. When a character puts me under house arrest, I have to remember that I can escape.

—MICHAEL CADNUM, *poet and novelist*

Openings and Endings

*Y*ou can't know a book until you come to the end of it, and then all the rest must be modified to fit that.

—MAXWELL PERKINS, *editor*

The first chapter is the last chapter in disguise.

—RICHARD PECK, *novelist*

First sentences are doors to worlds.

—URSULA K. LE GUIN, *novelist*

The awful thing about the first sentence of any book is that as soon as you've written it you realize this piece of work is not going to be the great thing that you envision.

—TOM WOLFE, *novelist*

The first line of a poem is a hawk which won't let go of its prey.

—GABRIEL PREIL, *poet*

Cross out every sentence until you come to one you cannot do without. That is your beginning.

—GARY PROVOST, *writing teacher*

You don't initiate a story until you know how you're going to end it. You don't start a dinner party conversation—"A funny thing happened to me on the way to La Guardia"—and not know what happened in La Guardia.

—JOHN IRVING, *novelist*

I always do the first line well, but I have trouble doing the others.

—MOLIÈRE, *playwright*

The trick is not a great beginning but a great middle.

—THOMAS TREBITSCH PARKER, *novelist*

My greatest fear in working is always the end. Lately I have taken to tricking myself into finishing by leaving a hole in the middle somewhere, then stitching the two pieces together—the Union Pacific approach.

—TWYLA THARP, *choreographer*

The only authentic ending is:
John and Mary die. John and Mary die. John and Mary die.
So much for endings. Beginnings are always more fun. True connoisseurs, however, are known to favor the stretch in between, since it's the hardest to do anything with.

—MARGARET ATWOOD, *novelist and poet*

The last third of the book only takes about 10 percent of the time. I don't know whether that's due to confidence or because the alternatives have been narrowed down.

—JOSEPH HELLER, *novelist*

There is conflict and conflict produces tension. And the solution to the problem releases tension and that is probably when the play should end.

—EDWARD ALBEE, *playwright*

Too many pieces finish long after the end.

—IGOR STRAVINSKY, *composer*

Not to write happy endings doesn't mean the writer doesn't believe in them.

—ROBERT CORMIER, *novelist*

I always wanted to write a book that ended with the word mayonnaise.

—RICHARD BRAUTIGAN, *novelist*

Researching, Revising and Re-envisioning

I saw the angel in the marble and I just chiseled till I set him free.
—MICHELANGELO, *sculptor*

In baseball, you only get three swings and you're out. In rewriting, you get almost as many swings as you want and you know, sooner or later, you'll hit the ball.

—NEIL SIMON, *playwright*

I love revisions. Where else in life can spilled milk be transformed into ice cream?

—KATHERINE PATERSON, *novelist*

Blot out, correct, insert, refine,
Enlarge, diminish, interline;
Be mindful, when Invention fails,
To scratch your Head and bite your Nails.

—JONATHAN SWIFT, *satirist, "On Poetry: A Rapsody"*

If I counted the pages I've torn up, of how many volumes am I the author?

—COLETTE, *novelist*

Writing a first draft is very much like watching a Polaroid develop. You can't—and, in fact, you're not supposed to—know exactly what the picture is going to look like until it has finished developing.

—ANNE LAMOTT, *novelist and essayist*

I used to be adjective-happy. Now I cut them with so much severity that I find I have to put a few adjectives back.

—FRANK YERBY, *novelist*

My efforts to cut out 50,000 words may sometimes result in my
adding 75,000.

—THOMAS WOLFE, *novelist*

One must be ruthless with one's own writing or someone else
will be.

—JOHN BERRYMAN, *poet*

Murder your darlings.

—ERIC HODGINS, *magazine publisher and novelist*

The hard work goes into the idea—fiddling with it and rejecting it and
loving it and hating it. I probably do 15 drafts for a book. Sometimes
I'm deliriously happy. Other times, I'm just wiped out.

—ERIC CARLE, *picture book writer and illustrator*

The idea of writing a first draft with the idea of revising the first draft
is repugnant to me. I have to play for keeps on every page.

—ROBERT PENN WARREN, *poet and novelist*

Few things are more interesting than revising. Having seen what you
said, you begin to discover what you meant. It's like psychoanalysis—
except it's free.

—ZIBBY ONEAL, *novelist*

I turn sentences around. That's my life. I write a sentence and then I turn it around. Then I look at it and I turn it around again.

—PHILIP ROTH, *novelist and short story writer*

I know my stuff all looks like it was rattled off in twenty-three seconds, but every word is a struggle—every sentence is like pangs of birth. *The Cat in the Hat* ended up taking well over a year.

—DR. SEUSS, *author and illustrator*

The unconscious creates, the ego edits.

—STANLEY KUNITZ, *poet*

The main reason for rewriting is not to achieve a smooth surface, but to discover the inner truth of your characters.

—SAUL BELLOW, *novelist*

There's an old cowboy's trick. The herd is coming through fast and one cowboy asks another how you estimate the number of cows so quickly. The other cowboy says: "it's very easy. You just count the number of hooves and divide by four." That's how you write a play: you do a lot of writing to figure out what the play's about and throw out three-quarters of it; then you write it again and look at it and find out what *that* play's about and throw out three-quarters of it; then you write it again.

—DAVID MAMET, *playwright*

Some women primp, I rewrite.

—FLORENCE KING, *essayist and critic*

I never found out the moon didn't come up in the west until I was a writer and Herschel Brickell, the literary critic, told me after I misplaced it in a story. He said valuable words to me about my new profession: "Always be sure you get the moon in the right part of the sky."

—EUDORA WELTY, *novelist and short story writer*

The wastepaper basket is a writer's best friend.

—ISAAC BASHEVIS SINGER, *novelist*

There are no first drafts in my life. An incinerator is a writer's best friend.

—THORNTON WILDER, *novelist and playwright*

I always try to write on the principle of the iceberg. There are seven-eighths of it under water for every part that shows.

—ERNEST HEMINGWAY, *novelist and short story writer*

I need to do a scene badly several times in order to end up doing it well.

—PETER HALL, *theater director*

My objective is to show what I found, not what I was looking for.

—PABLO PICASSO, *painter*

If it is possible to cut a word out, always cut it out.

—GEORGE ORWELL, *novelist and essayist*

I do what I consider to be 60% of the research; then I begin writing. It's when you write that you learn what you don't know—and what you need to find out.

—DAVID McCULLOUGH, *historian and biographer*

A wonderful writer/teacher named Rivers taught me the rule every reporter must know: Verify everything. If your mother says she loves you, get a second source.

—MARSHALL J. COOK, *writing teacher*

Facts and truth really don't have much to do with each other.

—WILLIAM FAULKNER, *novelist*

If it looks as if I worked on it, I go back and work some more.

—BETSY BYARS, *novelist*

The beautiful part of writing is that you don't have to get it right the first time, unlike, say, a brain surgeon.

—ROBERT CORMIER, *novelist*

Read over your compositions, and wherever you meet with a passage which you think is particularly fine, strike it out.

—SAMUEL JOHNSON, *critic and lexicographer*

In this act of creation and constant judgment of it as he is creating, the writer is like someone trying to measure a dream with a dissolving ruler.

—BERNARD MALAMUD, *novelist*

A poem may be worked over once it is in being, but may not be worried into being. It can never lose its sense of a meaning that once unfolded by surprise as it went.

—ROBERT FROST, *poet*

Writing is like getting married. One should never commit oneself until one is amazed at one's luck.

—IRIS MURDOCH, *novelist*

I don't think it ever hurts the writer to sort of stand back now and then and look at his stuff as if he were reading it instead of writing it.

—JAMES JONES, *novelist*

The last act of writing must be to become one's own reader. It is, I suppose, a schizophrenic process. To begin passionately and to end critically, to begin hot and to end cold; and, more important, to try to be passion-hot and critic-cold at the same time.

—JOHN CIARDI, *poet and essayist*

It is in order to shine sooner that authors refuse to rewrite. Despicable. Begin again.

—ALBERT CAMUS, *novelist*

How does one know which is the final version of a story? In the same way the cook knows when the soup is ready, this is a trade secret that does not obey the laws of reason but the magic of instinct.

—GABRIEL GARCÍA MÁRQUEZ, *novelist*

Only God gets it right the first time.

—STEPHEN KING, *novelist*

Submitting the Work

In literature, as in love, we are astonished at what is chosen by others.

—ANDRÉ MAUROIS, *biographer and novelist*

Every time you submit a manuscript to a magazine or a publishing house, it's like going out on a blind date. You are asking a complete stranger to do an instant evaluation of your total worth as a human being.

—DAN GREENBURG, *journalist and humorist*

My twelve-year-old son has decided to take up a career in the theater. I told him that going to auditions reminds me an awful lot of submitting manuscripts and I don't understand why he thinks this is fun. At least I have never had a book rejected because I was too fat for the part. As far as I know.

—MARGARET BECHARD, *novelist*

This is what they'll put on my tombstone: HE WAS ONLY HERE ON SPEC!

—LOUIS PHILLIPS, *poet and playwright*

The submission process can sometimes make one feel like Dorothy at the gates of the Emerald City—that you're at the mercy of a mercurial gatekeeper who is apparently determined to thwart you, no matter how hard you try. That getting in, in short, will be next to impossible.

—LISA BERNSTEIN, *editor*

The way to write a great play is not the problem at all. The problem is how do you get past the frauds and all-around incompetents who from sheer force of ambition occupy all the positions of power, and prevent, obstruct, neutralize, distort or otherwise prohibit the performance of a great play after it is written.

—WILLIAM SAROYAN, *playwright*

A query letter is like a fishing expedition; don't put too much bait on your hook or you'll lose your quarry. Be brief and be tantalizing!

—JANE VON MEHREN, *editor*

An ambitious unknown writer struggles against large odds. Publishers can afford the gamble, but most writers can't.

—MICHAEL NORMAN, *journalist*

Show your work to no one, not to friend, nor spouse, nor anyone. The publisher or producer, eventually, will say yes or no, which are the only words you need to hear.

—FAY WELDON, *novelist*

The first book I ever wrote was the best-selling book of the year, and the second book dropped dead. What can we learn from this? Absolutely nothing. But if you keep on submitting and never give up, the chances are that someday somebody will eventually buy your work. Unless they don't.

—DAN GREENBURG, *journalist and humorist*

All human wisdom is summed up in two words: wait and hope.

—ALEXANDRE DUMAS, *novelist*

"HE SMOKES A CIGAR
AND GETS 15%"

Agents and Contracts

The publishing process moves at the speed of a glacier. An agent's
role is to be a match, melting a little path.

—SUSAN COHEN, *literary agent*

You put a publisher among a bunch of authors. It's like
a fox in a chicken coop. My job is to be the
fox patrol.

—KENNETH DAVID BURROWS, *literary attorney*

Your agent is your lifeline, your reality check, and your best friend.

—RITA MAE BROWN, *novelist*

If you're an unknown author, the agent's reputation is the first thing an editor knows about you.

—LORI PERKINS, *agent*

Agent: Obscene word.

—GUSTAVE FLAUBERT, *novelist*

The earth has circled the sun many times since a well-known publisher could display on his office wall a beautifully wrought needlepoint sampler reading, "The relationship between publisher and agent is that of knife to throat."

—ALAN D. WILLIAMS, *editor*

Knowing that most authors write for love, publishers [in earlier times] tended to assume that they didn't need to write for money.

—RICHARD CURTIS, *agent*

A good publisher cannot afford the luxury of being color-blind. He must be able to distinguish between black ink and red.

—M. LINCOLN SCHUSTER, *publisher*

The worst thing you can have in a contract is ambiguity.

—MARSHALL NELSON, *attorney*

Do you know what an agent does? He smokes a cigar, takes your writing, tries to sell it, never does, and gets 15%. That's what an agent does.

—MAX STRAVINSKY, in Maira Kalman's
Max Makes a Million

Editors and Editing

*Y*ou have the right to not change anything, but don't be a fool.
Change things if somebody else is right. But if you do change
something because somebody else is right, you must instantly take credit
for it yourself. That's very important.

—EDWARD ALBEE, *playwright*

English publishers say that American editors nit-pick, but I
like that. I say, "Better for the publisher to nit-pick than
the reviewer."

—LADY ANTONIA FRASER, *biographer and novelist*

Please don't change my lines willy-nilly, it makes me cry. If you were a writer, you'd be a writer. And if you are a writer, then change your own lines, not mine.

—CHRISTOPHER DURANG, *playwright*

The book belongs to the author. An editor at most releases energy. He creates nothing.

—MAXWELL PERKINS, *editor*

Going over a manuscript line by line has as little to do with pleasure as does the creation of those lines. More important is that the reader be pleased by the result.

—ARTHUR PLOTNIK, *editor*

Relationships have broken down when an author and an editor became too intimate. When genuine friendship occurs, and it does, of course, it can be wonderful. It had better be genuine; it is certain to be tested.

—SAMUEL S. VAUGHAN, *editor*

No one wants advice—only corroboration.

—JOHN STEINBECK, *novelist*

Pray you find a good editor, because, though you may be good, you are unlikely to be perfect.

—THOMAS MCCORMACK, *editor and publisher*

Humility is all in the face of a good editor; it's too easy to fall in love with your own words.

—ZIBBY ONEAL, *novelist*

If it weren't for editors and designers with the gift for giving shape, writers could be frizzled to bits with overloads of possibilities.

—PEGGY THOMSON, *nonfiction writer*

I have a crime writer friend who thinks that the ideal editor is someone who likes every word you write. I disagree. I like someone who, with a good heart, attacks, who really sees to the essence of what's wrong.

—WILLIAM BAYER, *novelist*

Don't pass judgment on a manuscript *as it is,* but *as it can be made to be.*

—M. LINCOLN SCHUSTER, *editor*

Beware the editor who claims that line-editing isn't important. It's like a fisherman who doesn't bother to mend his nets.

—LISA BERNSTEIN, *editor*

A writer doesn't die of heart failure, but of typographical errors.

—ISAAC BASHEVIS SINGER, *novelist*

The best editors advocate the sometimes conflicting interests of three parties: publisher, author, and consumer. . . . Advocacy within the bounds of solvency.

—ARTHUR PLOTNIK, *editor*

The effective editor is on comfortable terms with God and Mammon.

—GERALD HOWARD, *editor*

A good many young writers make the mistake of enclosing a stamped, self-addressed envelope big enough for the manuscript to come back in. This is too much of a temptation to the editor.

—RING LARDNER, *short story writer*

I've always thought it unfair that—although editors and art directors are often central figures in the creation of a book—they are never credited, not on the cover, not on the title page, not even on the copyright page.

—NEIL WALDMAN, *author and illustrator*

Always remember that if editors were so damned smart, they would know how to dress.

—DAVE BARRY, *humorist*

An editor is a person who knows precisely what he wants but isn't quite sure.

—WALTER DAVENPORT, *novelist*

My definition of a good editor is a man I think charming, who sends me large checks, praises my work, my physical beauty, and my sexual prowess, and who has a stranglehold on the publisher and the bank.

—JOHN CHEEVER, *novelist and short story writer*

"EACH ONE WAS A LITTLE DOOM"

Rejection Letters

*N*othing stinks like a pile of unpublished writing.

—SYLVIA PLATH, *poet*

Writers are always sending themselves rejection letters, as the
late George P. Elliot observed, to this sentence and that paragraph,
to this initial characterization and that turn of the story, or,
heartbreak time, to the story that has eluded months of tracking
it, the hundred pages of a novel that has come to a
dead stop.

—TED SOLOTAROFF, *editor*

If it's approval you want, don't be a writer.

—FAY WELDON, *novelist*

Rejections give me the shivers and always will. Each one was a little doom. Had a personal fight with each one. And it's such a short time ago and it may be again.

—JOHN STEINBECK, *novelist*

The trouble was, he had expected praise. It was an occupational disease of novelists. No matter how nasty your themes, you still wanted to be loved for them.

—RICHARD HALL, *novelist and critic*

If the writer has a good idea but no ability to execute it, then nothing would compel me to buy it.

—KATE DUFFY, *editor*

It is impossible to sell animal stories in the U.S.A.

—REJECTION LETTER FOR GEORGE ORWELL'S *ANIMAL FARM*

"CREATE YOUR OWN DEMAND"

Getting Published

*P*ublishers don't nurse you; they buy and sell you.

—P. D. JAMES, *novelist*

No author is a man of genius to his publisher.

—HEINRICH HEINE, *poet*

There's a marvelous peace in not being published.

—J. D. SALINGER, *novelist and short story writer*

I object to publishers: the one service they have done me is to teach me to do without them. All that is necessary in the production of a book is an author and a bookseller, without any intermediate parasite.

—GEORGE BERNARD SHAW, *playwright*

Many authors feel that they do not get fair treatment from publishers. I think they are mistaken, but I have never found a way of persuading them of that fact.

—JOHN FARRAR, *publisher*

In the rage for cheapness we have sacrificed everything for slop, and a dainty bit of bookmaking is like a jewel in the swine's snout.

—PUBLISHERS WEEKLY, 1884

It is a meretricious view that writers and editors are "creative" and that production and sales are "servicing." Creativity has to be at the heart of all publishing.

—PETER MAYER, *publisher*

Publishers are like wives; everyone wants somebody else's—but when you have them where's the difference?

—NORMAN DOUGLAS, *novelist*

When offers are coming in, you want to be professional, but what you really want to ask is: "Do you really like it?"

—JOE KANON, *first-time novelist and former publisher*

You have to remember that nobody ever wants a new writer. You have to create your own demand.

—DORIS LESSING, *novelist*

I have a certain conception of the right relationship between a writer and publisher, a relationship that might be, at its best, a kind of intellectual marriage.

—SHERWOOD ANDERSON, *short story writer and novelist*

Not everything that is thought should be expressed. Not everything that is expressed should be expressed verbally. Not everything that is expressed verbally should be written. Not everything that is written should be published.

—ISRAEL SALANTER, *rabbi*

Someone was going to print my book. Someone was going to sell my book. Someone was going to buy my book. I couldn't talk. I couldn't think. I couldn't breathe. The world was a fuzzy kind place. The world was O.K. Not just O.K. but A.O.K.

—MAX STRAVINSKY, in Maira Kalman's
Max Makes a Million

Publication is not all that it is cracked up to be. But writing is. It's like discovering that while you thought you needed the tea ceremony for the caffeine, what you really needed was the tea ceremony. The act of writing turns out to be its own reward.

—ANNE LAMOTT, *novelist and essayist*

Marketing, Advertising, and Publicity

*A*nyone can print a book; the trick is to get someone to read it.

—PETER MAYER, *publisher*

I often think how shocked authors would be if they listened
to the salesmen selling their books. They've worked for a year on
their book—two years, three years, maybe longer. And there it is.
A word or two and the decision is made. I don't think many authors
could stand it.

—GEORGE SCHEER, *sales representative*

The shelf life of the average trade book is somewhere between milk and yogurt.

—CALVIN TRILLIN, *humorist*

Publishing literary novels is like sailing a small craft. Either you catch the wind or you have to paddle very hard.

—NAN TALESE, *editor*

Advertising is the rattling of a stick inside a swill bucket.

—GEORGE ORWELL, *novelist and essayist*

It's obviously important to support first novelists—or where will second books come from?

—OTTO PENZLER, *publisher and bookseller*

The whole question of conflict between culture and commerce only comes up when the strategies have been inadequate.

—PETER MAYER, *publisher*

I don't promote my books. I never have—I just think my time is better spent writing the best book I can.

—JUDITH MCNAUGHT, *best-selling romance writer*

Writers must get past the creative process and understand that what they're selling is a product.

—CAROL STACY, *publisher*

Publishing is a very mysterious business. It is hard to predict what kind of sale or reception a book will have, and advertising seems to do very little good.

—THOMAS WOLFE, *novelist*

Create the best in anything, and there's usually a market for it.

—RICHARD BRANSON, *international entrepreneur*

I belong to a vanishing breed that thinks a writer should be read and not heard, let alone seen.

—WILLIAM GADDIS, *novelist*

Wanting to know an author because you like his work is like wanting to know a duck because you like paté.

—ADAM BEGLEY, *journalist and critic*

The Audience

I have never met an author who admitted that people did not buy his book because it was dull.

—W. Somerset Maugham, *novelist*

Thirty percent of Americans may *write* poetry, but I doubt that thirty percent *read* poetry, even their own.

—David Lehman, *poet*

Publishing a volume of verse is like dropping a rose petal down the Grand Canyon and waiting for the echo.

—Don Marquis, *poet and humorist*

Whether an audience *likes* it is less important than whether they *understand* it.

—STEPHEN SONDHEIM, *composer and lyricist*

Imagine the text not as a story, but as a score; imagine the reader as its performer.

—LEONARD FEIN, *journalist*

The one thing art cannot afford to be is private. It is created to be pleasure.

—FERNANDO BOTERO, *painter and sculptor*

The audience is the reason you're performing.

—DARCI KISTLER, *dancer*

People who don't like detective stories are anarchists.

—REX STOUT, *mystery writer*

There is a perception that men's books are for everyone and women's books are for women, and we want to change that.

—KATE MOSS, *novelist*

Anybody who shifts gears when he writes for children is likely to wind up stripping his gears.

—E. B. WHITE, *essayist and novelist*

A book is not harmless merely because no one is consciously offended by it.

—T. S. ELIOT, *poet*

Even the ancient mariner, with his wonderful tale, succeeded in stopping only one of three! No book is for everybody.

—LEON GARFIELD, *novelist*

An author ought to write for the youth of his own generation, the critic of the next, and the schoolmaster of ever afterwards.

—F. SCOTT FITZGERALD, *novelist*

You have to make your vision apparent by shock—to the hard of hearing you shout and for the almost blind you draw large and startling figures.

—FLANNERY O'CONNOR, *novelist and short story writer*

The reading of a poem, a poetry reading, is not a spectacle, nor can it be passively received. It's an exchange of electrical currents through language.

—ADRIENNE RICH, *poet and essayist*

Reviews and Criticism

*Y*ou mustn't fall into the trap of assuming that because nobody likes what you have done it is very good. Sometimes people don't like what you've done because it is terrible.

—EDWARD ALBEE, *playwright*

Your writing is never as good as you hoped; but never as bad as you feared.

—BERTRAND RUSSELL, *philosopher*

The gifted young writer has to learn through adversity to separate rejection of one's work from self-rejection, and with respect to the latter, self-criticism (otherwise known as revision and what one might call re-envision) from self-distrust.

—TED SOLOTAROFF, *editor*

The great critic is an artist as well. He tells us what he thinks is good, he tells us why he thinks so, and he performs both functions in such a way that we are excited by his manner while convinced by his argument.

—WINTON DEAN, *critic*

The philistinism of interpretation is more rife in literature than in any other art. The function of criticism should be to show *how it is what it is,* even *that it is what it is,* rather than show *what it means.*

—SUSAN SONTAG, *critic and essayist*

The new generation isn't really critics. They're literary reporters.

—ROGER STRAUS, *publisher*

The prevailing ethos of literary criticism, especially in England, inclines to scalping, where the clever bow to the clever, where the merest manifestation of feeling is pilloried and where consideration of language itself is zero.

—EDNA O'BRIEN, *novelist and short story writer*

When big analytic tools are brought to bear on decidedly slight materials, it's like watching envelopes being opened by lasers or hot dogs set in their buns using cranes.

—WALTER KIRN, *book reviewer*

You don't love to read the reviews that are terrible. On the other hand, if you really believe in what you do, you don't believe the review.

—ROY LICHTENSTEIN, *painter*

I don't take to praise and fawning, because I feel that if you accept that, you have to accept it when someone calls you a pile of shit, which I also don't accept.

—MORRISSEY, *pop star*

I don't read my reviews; I measure them.

—H. G. WELLS, *novelist*

A poet can survive everything but a misprint.

—OSCAR WILDE, *dramatist and critic*

Literary critics are people who can't create themselves, so they try to disgrace talented writers. To praise a writer, all they need is a few sentences; but to tear him to shreds provides wonderful material for a long essay.

—ISAAC BASHEVIS SINGER, *novelist*

If you don't like my book, write your own. If you don't think you can write a novel, that ought to tell you something. If you think you can, do. No excuses. If you still don't like my novels, find a book you do like. Life is too short to be miserable. If you like my novels, I commend your good taste.

—RITA MAE BROWN, *novelist*

I never read a book before reviewing it; it prejudices a man so.

—SYDNEY SMITH, *clergyman and humorist*

The critic works on behalf of the audience: you're trying to help the audience toward the artist and the artist toward the audience.

—ARLENE CROCE, *dance critic*

A bad review is even less important than whether it is raining in Patagonia.

—IRIS MURDOCH, *novelist*

There is no such thing as a moral or an immoral book. Books are well written, or badly written. That is all.

—OSCAR WILDE, *dramatist and critic*

Censorship is always a power trip. What is at the bottom is about who's on top.

—STEPHEN KING, *novelist*

Damn all expurgated books, the dirtiest book of all is the
expurgated book.

—WALT WHITMAN, *poet*

Pulling books from library shelves in order to protect children from
satanic abuse makes about as much sense as trying to protect boys and
girls from molesters by outlawing trenchcoats.

—KERRY LEIGH ELLISON, *educator and library consultant*

Book reviews are sort of autobiographies, diaries of our tastes and
predilections.

—LAURIE STONE, *reviewer*

I wish critics would judge me as an author, not as a woman.

—CHARLOTTE BRONTË, *novelist*

With white writers there are a lot of gray areas. There are commercial
writers, literary writers, genre writers. But if it's black and it holds a
pencil—that's the category.

—WANDA COLEMAN, *poet and novelist*

John Ciardi was outspokenly critical of traditional poetry aimed at
youngsters, which struck him as "written by a sponge dipped in warm
milk and sprinkled with sugar."

—ROBERT O. BOORSTIN, in *New York Times* obituary

A Viennese novelist, a refugee, said that he had lost his country, his home, his language, but that he had had at least one good fortune: he had not been reviewed by me.

—DIANA TRILLING, *critic*

Dr. Seuss is remembered for the murder of Dick and Jane, which was a mercy killing of the highest order.

—ANNA QUINDLEN, *columnist and novelist*

If one person says you're a donkey, don't mind. If two say so, be worried. If three say so, go buy yourself a saddle.

—YIDDISH PROVERB

Failing and Succeeding

Keep two truths in your pocket, and take them out according to the need of the moment. Let one be: for my sake was the world created. And the other: I am dust and ashes.

—SIMCHA BUNIM, *rabbi*

Fate keeps on happening.

—ANITA LOOS, *novelist and screenwriter*

Don't look back. Something might be gaining on you.

—SATCHEL PAIGE, *baseball player*

Stop! Really stop when someone is complimenting you. Even if it's painful and you are not used to it, just keep breathing, listen, and let yourself take it in. *Feel* how good it is. Build up a tolerance for positive, honest support.

—NATALIE GOLDBERG, *poet and writing teacher*

Balanchine wanted to get me not to worry about making a masterpiece every time. "Just keep making ballets," he used to say, "and every once in a while one will be a masterpiece."

—JEROME ROBBINS, *choreographer*

No one can make you feel inferior without your consent.

—ELEANOR ROOSEVELT, *human rights activist and American First Lady*

This thing we call "failure" is not the falling down, but the staying down.

—MARY PICKFORD, *actor*

Mazel [luck] is the imp of metaphysics.

—REBECCA GOLDSTEIN, *novelist and short story writer*

Never stop daring to hang yourself.

—BETTE DAVIS, *actor*

At the end of every year, I'd take stock. As long as the songs I'd written that year were better than the ones that had come before, that sense of progress would get me through, and give me the will to tough it out.

—BILL MORRISSEY, *songwriter*

You can't build a reputation on what you are *going* to do.

—HENRY FORD, *inventor and businessman*

The one whose chariot is driven by Reason
And holds the reins of his Mind,
Reaches the end of the journey.

THE UPANISHADS

If we make use of a talent it is only because we make use of another talent, a talent for using talents.

—A. A. MILNE, *poet and novelist*

It is important to possess a short-term pessimism and a long-term optimism.

—ADRIENNE RICH, *poet and essayist*

If you're going to do good work, the work has to scare you.

—ANDRÉ PREVIN, *composer and conductor*

You can only be as good as you dare to be bad.

—JOHN BARRYMORE, *actor*

Failure is apt to produce self-pity and it's been my experience that self-pity can be very productive.

—IRWIN SHAW, *novelist*

It is never too late to be what you might have been.

—GEORGE ELIOT, *novelist*

The day-to-day failure is, of course, the failure upstairs in your study that no one else knows about.

—JIM SHEPARD, *novelist*

I dread success. To have succeeded is to have finished one's business on earth, like the male spider, who is killed by the female the moment he has succeeded in his courtship. I like a state of continual becoming, with a goal in front and not behind.

—GEORGE BERNARD SHAW, *playwright and socialist*

The "let's see" attitude is enticing to certain minds, like skydiving. I don't scorn daring, but still I want to see craft in packing the parachute and picking a landing area. I recall one famous writer of a generation ago who was resolutely against planning anything. "If I knew what was going to happen I'd be too bored to write it." His career was marked, after early success, by constant failure.

—THOMAS McCORMACK, *editor and publisher*

If anything can stop you from becoming a writer, let it. If nothing can stop you, do it and you'll make it.

—JOHN DODD, *publisher*

As the world smashes you down—as it dances on your grave—it unleashes the creative force.

—KAY LARSON, *art critic*

The only way to escape the personal corruption of praise is to go on working.

—ALBERT EINSTEIN, *scientist and philosopher*

We have an idea that success is a happy occasion. Success can also be lonely, isolating, disappointing. . . . I tell myself, "Natalie, this book is done. You will write another one."

—NATALIE GOLDBERG, *poet and writing teacher*

Never look back. That way you fall down stairs.

—RUDOLF NUREYEV, *dancer*

Mastery is not something that strikes in an instant, like a thunderbolt, but a gathering power that moves steadily through time, like weather.

—JOHN GARDNER, *novelist and writing teacher*

Never hope more than you work.

—Rita Mae Brown, *novelist*

I suppose that there are endeavors in which self-confidence is even more important than it is in writing—tightrope walking comes immediately to mind—but it's difficult for me to think of anybody producing much writing if his confidence is completely shot.

—Calvin Trillin, *journalist and humorist*

All you need is fifty lucky breaks.

—Walter Matthau, *actor*

Professional Jealousy and Other Cranky Comments

$\mathcal{T}$his is not a novel to be tossed aside lightly. It should be thrown with great force.

—DOROTHY PARKER, *humorist*

An insufficient talent is the cruelest of all temptations.

—GEORGE MOORE, *novelist and critic*

Unless you think you can do better than Tolstoy, we don't need you.

—JAMES MICHENER, *novelist*

The immature poet imitates; the mature poet plagiarizes.

—T. S. ELIOT, *poet*

There can hardly be a stranger commodity in the world than books. Printed by people who don't understand them; sold by people who don't understand them; bound, criticized and read by people who don't understand them; and now even written by people who don't understand them.

—GEORG CHRISTOPH LICHTENBERG, *editor*

One must have a heart of stone to read the death of Little Nell [in Dickens's *The Old Curiosity Shop*] without laughing.

—OSCAR WILDE, *dramatist and critic*

Authors are sometimes like tomcats: they distrust all the other toms, but they are kind to kittens.

—MALCOLM COWLEY, *novelist and critic*

Very few people possess true artistic ability. It is therefore both unseemly and unproductive to irritate the situation by making an effort. If you have a burning, restless urge to write or paint, simply eat something sweet and the feeling will pass.

—FRAN LEBOWITZ, *humorist*

The best part of the fiction in many novels is the notice that the characters are purely imaginary.

—FRANKLIN PIERCE ADAMS, *columnist*

The trouble with the publishing business is that too many people who have half a mind to write a book do so.

—WILLIAM TARG, *literary agent*

Everywhere I go I'm asked if I think the university stifles writers. My opinion is that they don't stifle enough of them. There's many a bestseller that could have been prevented by a good teacher.

—FLANNERY O'CONNOR, *novelist and short story writer*

If it were thought that anything I wrote was influenced by Robert Frost, I would take that particular work of mine, shred it, and flush it down the toilet, hoping not to clog the pipes.

—JAMES DICKEY, *poet and novelist*

Shaw fills his nothingness with incisive speculation; Beckett raised nothingness to fierce, tragicomic heights. But the nothingness of Albee's plays is petty, self-indulgent, stationary. Albee's nothing is as dull as anything.

—JOHN SIMON, *critic*

Most writers regard the truth as their most valuable possession, and therefore are most economical in its use.

—MARK TWAIN, *humorist*

Some editors are failed writers, but so are most writers.

—T. S. ELIOT, *poet*

Every word she writes is a lie, including "and" and "the."

—MARY McCARTHY, *novelist, on Lillian Hellman, playwright*

Real seriousness in regard to writing is one of two absolute necessities. The other, unfortunately, is talent.

—ERNEST HEMINGWAY, *novelist and short story writer*

If you ask someone, "Can you play the violin?" and he says, "I don't know, I've not tried, perhaps I can," you laugh at him. Whereas about writing, people always say: "I don't know, I have not tried," as though one had only to try and one would become a writer.

—LEO TOLSTOY, *novelist*

In America only the successful writer is important, in France all writers are important, in England no writer is important and in Australia you have to explain what a writer is.

—GEOFFREY COTTERELL, *novelist*

Enemies are so stimulating.

—KATHARINE HEPBURN, *actor*

One hour a day, you have to hate everyone.

—MARTIN AMIS, *novelist*

Fame and Fortune

*W*hen you write you want fame, fortune and personal satisfaction. You want to write what you want to write and to feel that it's good and to sell millions of copies of it and have everybody whose opinion you value think it's good, and you want this to go on for hundreds of years. Anything less is kind of piddling.

—DASHIELL HAMMETT, *novelist*

There's no money in poetry, but then there's no poetry in money either.

—ROBERT GRAVES, *poet and novelist*

There must be more to life than having everything.

—MAURICE SENDAK, *writer and illustrator*

I don't have any sense of the commercial marketplace. I feel that when you start to think, Will this sell?, that's death.

—MICHAEL CRICHTON, *best-selling novelist*

Talent is a kind of wealth, and if you find it under your pillow some morning, you are as surprised as anybody else.

—GARRISON KEILLOR, *writer and performer*

If you would not be forgotten as soon as you are dead and rotten, either write things worth reading, or do things worth the writing.

—BENJAMIN FRANKLIN, *statesman and inventor*

If you want to be famous, keep typing!

—CLAIRE M. SMITH, *literary agent*

What good is happiness? It can't buy money.

—ANONYMOUS

Money was a virus. Money could make you sick. Worse, money corrupted words.

—BILL HENDERSON, *editor and publisher*

Money isn't everything as long as you have enough.

—MALCOLM FORBES, *businessman*

Boots, the cat owned by Laura Tucker, recording secretary of the Association of Authors Representatives, recently gave birth to twins. She named one Royalty Statement because it was very late and much smaller than expected. She called the second Ungrateful Author because it bites the hand that feeds it.

—*AAR NEWSLETTER*

The playwright needs a producer who will stick by him through thin and thin.

—LOUIS PHILLIPS, *poet and playwright*

Money is better than poverty, if only for financial reasons.

—WOODY ALLEN, *filmmaker and humorist*

There are probably no more than ten people who can earn a living on the revenue from books alone.

—ELLEN GEIGER, *literary agent*

Only in dreams are carrots as big as bears.

—YIDDISH PROVERB

When the Library of Congress talk and reception was over, with, I must own, acclamation, back at our hotel I said to James, "I don't want to do this any more."

For a moment he was stunned. . . . "You mean, one can't go any higher than this. Is that it?" he asked.

"No," I said, "I mean it isn't writing."

—RUMER GODDEN, *novelist*

My speed depends on the state of my bank account.

—MICKEY SPILLANE, *novelist*

It took me fifteen years to discover that I had no talent for writing, but I couldn't give it up because by that time I was too famous.

—ROBERT BENCHLEY, *humorist*

Don't be humble. You're not that great.

—GOLDA MEIR, *Israeli prime minister*

One must avoid ambition in order to write. Otherwise something else is the goal: some kind of power beyond the power of language. And the power of language, it seems to me, is the only kind of power a writer is entitled to.

—CYNTHIA OZICK, *novelist*

When I am dead, I hope it may be said:
"His sins were scarlet, but his books were read."

—HILAIRE BELLOC, *poet and satirist*

Whom the gods wish to destroy they first call promising.

—CYRIL CONNOLLY, *novelist and critic*

Li Po wrote poems on rice paper and floated them down rivers until they sank out of sight. Contemporary poets publish their poems in little magazines. The results are much the same.

—LOUIS PHILLIPS, *poet and playwright*

Keep a diary and one day it'll keep you.

—MAE WEST, *actor and scriptwriter*

The canon is not made by anybody except other poets.

—HELEN VENDLER, *poetry critic and teacher*

When you can see the bandwagon, it's already gone.

—WILLEM DE KOONING, *painter*

Just you wait, I'll become famous after I'm dead about ten years.

—JIM THOMPSON, *novelist*

It occurred to me that perhaps writing a book was not as entertaining an activity as signing the contract to write it.

—PETE DEXTER, *novelist*

I don't think living in cellars and starving is any better for an artist than it is for anybody else.

—KATHERINE ANNE PORTER, *novelist*

"GIVE IT ALL, GIVE IT NOW"

On to the Next Book

One of the few things I know about writing is this: spend it all, shoot it, play it, lose it, all, right away, every time. Do not hoard what seems good for a better place in the book, or for another book; give it, give it all, give it now.

—ANNIE DILLARD, *naturalist and essayist*

At my first literary luncheon, a woman asked me with absolute sincerity, "How does it feel to have written your best book first?"

—AMY TAN, *novelist*

The fulfilled expectation is almost disappointment, for only anticipated pleasure is really pleasure; in pleasure which is fulfilled its opposite is already stirring.

—ALBERT SCHWEITZER, *philosopher*

I feel somewhat at a loss, aimless and foolishly sentimental, and disconnected, when I've finished one work and haven't yet become absorbed in another.

—MARIANNE MOORE, *poet*

I'm stacking up stuff about the story and thinking about these people—I've known who they are for a while, I see them, but they haven't started talking to me yet. It's like a picture that's out of focus. I don't force things on my characters; I wait and watch them grow.

—TERRY MCMILLAN, *novelist*

When the book is finished, it seems as if the story had always existed. But when it's time to begin the next book, I recognize with trepidation, almost fear, that this new story has to be pulled from my brain and my bones, and even the texture of the paper, and the sharpness of the pencil doesn't comfort me—until suddenly the character begins to emerge . . . a turn of his head perhaps, the way he walks down the street circling the trees. . . . It is at that moment I feel anything is possible, and I know the elation of being a writer.

—PATRICIA REILLY GIFF, *novelist and picture book writer*

And now a new work begins . . . tentatively, uncertainly . . . but in full knowledge that in the working process there will be comprehension, insight, awareness, intuition, and all that is needed to create.

—ANN SCHWENINGER, *picture book writer and illustrator*

A shoemaker when he has finished one pair of shoes does not sit down and contemplate his work in idle satisfaction. The shoemaker who so indulged himself would be without wages half his time. It is the same with a professional writer of books. Having made up my mind that I could be really happy only when I was at work, I had now quite accustomed myself to begin a second pair as soon as the first was out of hand.

—ANTHONY TROLLOPE, *novelist*

Of making many books, there is no end.

—ECCLESIASTES 12:12

I don't think there is a "next" book. Does a growing tree go on to the next branch? Readers who compare novels, and think of one book as having unity entirely apart from the previous works, are misunderstanding what takes place. I believe all novels are chapters in a Big Novel we are working on, although the characteristics of the books may be very different. I think there is writing going on all the time, somewhere in our minds.

—MICHAEL CADNUM, *poet and novelist*

The dogs bark, but the caravan moves on.

—ANDRÉ GIDE, *novelist*

Why Write?

The sheer pleasure of telling a story may be the human condition
that most resembles levitation.

—GABRIEL GARCÍA MÁRQUEZ, *novelist*

If I did not work, these worlds would perish.

—*BHAGAVAD GITA*

I can't understand why a person will take a year to write a novel when he
can easily buy one for a few dollars.

—FRED ALLEN, *humorist*

Writing is the only thing that, when I do it, I don't feel I should be doing something else.

—GLORIA STEINEM, *journalist and feminist*

I feel disturbed and upset if I'm not writing. I'm desperate to work every day.

—ALICE HOFFMAN, *novelist*

It's more exciting to write a novel than to run a country.

—AMOS OZ, *novelist and essayist*

Yes, writers could help people in trouble, using their power with words and the influence they had earned. After all, hadn't President Hoover said, "What this country needs is a great poem, something to lift people out of fear and selfishness. Sometimes a great poem can do more than legislation."

—MILTON MELTZER, *biographer and historian*

A great writer is, so to speak, a second government in his country. And for that reason no regime has ever loved great writers, only minor ones.

—ALEKSANDR SOLZHENITSYN, *novelist*

Draw your chair up close to the edge of the precipice, and I'll tell you a story.

—F. SCOTT FITZGERALD, *novelist*

Our lives aren't scripted, they're chaotic. That's why people enjoy art, not just narrative, but paintings and music, too. It's about giving order to what everybody knows does not have order at all.

—STEPHEN SONDHEIM, *composer and lyricist*

I'm not sure a bad person can write a good book. If art doesn't make us better, then what on earth is it for?

—ALICE WALKER, *novelist and poet*

Ah, to have your name in print! There are certain people who commit a crime for that pleasure alone.

—GUSTAVE FLAUBERT, *novelist*

To make us feel small in the right way is a function of art. Men can only make us feel small in the wrong way.

—E. M. FORSTER, *novelist*

It's an act of faith to be a writer in a postliterate world.

—RITA MAE BROWN, *novelist*

The world is complete without us. Intolerable fact. To which the poet responds by rebelling, wanting to prove otherwise.

—LOUISE GLÜCK, *poet*

The morning is greying with an unwritten poem. An attack of perhaps.

—GABRIEL PREIL, *poet*

How do I know what I think until I see what I say?

—E. M. FORSTER, *novelist*

Ink runs from the corners of my mouth.
There is no happiness like mine.
I have been eating poetry.

—MARK STRAND, *poet, "Eating Poetry"*

Writing well is a *pleasure*. Putting your feelings on paper, in coherent and forceful terms, is also one of the finest of all forms of therapy.

—CHARLES MCCABE, *journalist*

Poetry will lead to an understanding of the world.

—YEVGENY YEVTUSHENKO, *poet*

Writing is a form of personal freedom. It frees us from the mass identity we see in the making all around us. In the end, writers will write not to be outlaw heroes of some underculture but mainly to save themselves, to survive as individuals.

—DON DELILLO, *novelist*

I always tell people that I became a writer not because I went to school but because my mother took me to the library. I wanted to become a writer so I could have my name in the card catalog.

—SANDRA CISNEROS, *poet and fiction writer*

Any artist is the bringer of light.

—RUDOLF NUREYEV, *dancer*

I'm writing out of desperation. I felt compelled to write to make sense of it to myself—so I don't end up saying peculiar things like "I'm black and I'm proud." I write so I don't end up as a set of slogans and clichés.

—JAMAICA KINCAID, *novelist*

Many people believe that stories are told to put people to sleep. I tell mine to wake them up.

—NACHMAN OF BRATSLAV, *rabbi*

I want to live other lives. I've never quite believed that one chance is all I get. Writing is my way of getting other chances.

—ANNE TYLER, *novelist*

If you can't annoy somebody, there is little point in writing.

—KINGSLEY AMIS, *novelist*

People want to know why I do this, why I write such gross stuff. I like to tell them I have the heart of a small boy—and I keep it in a jar on my desk.

—STEPHEN KING, *author of horror novels*

You climb a long ladder until you see over the roof, or over the clouds. You are writing a book.

—ANNIE DILLARD, *naturalist and essayist*

It's a little mad, but I believe I am many people. When I am writing a poem, I feel I am the person who should have written it.

—ANNE SEXTON, *poet*

If I knew what the meanings of my books were, I wouldn't have bothered to write them.

—MARGARET DRABBLE, *novelist*

Writing is making sense of life. You work your whole life and perhaps you've made sense of one small area.

—NADINE GORDIMER, *novelist*

Life is just particles and waves until we make a story out of it.

—ALBERT MURRAY, *novelist and critic*

You become a writer because you need to become a writer—nothing else. Any work that you do that isn't writing is taking you away from writing.

—GRACE PALEY, *short story writer and poet*

I try to open a path through that maze, to put a little order in that chaos, to make life more bearable. When I write, I describe life as I would like it to be.

—ISABEL ALLENDE, *novelist*

When my mother was dying of cancer, she said, "Son, am I in your new book? . . . Don't make me like this. Make me beautiful. Promise me you will make me beautiful." After that moment I loved being a Southern writer. I said, "Mom, I'm going to make you so beautiful. Because you taught me right and raised me right, I can lift you off that bed and I can send you dancing. And I can make you beautiful again for everybody in the world." And my mother said, "I want Meryl Streep to play the role."

—PAT CONROY, *novelist*

Then he said to Scheherazade: "Sister, for the sake of Allah, tell us a story that will help pass the night."

—*THE ARABIAN NIGHTS*

When I write, it feels like I'm carving bone. It feels like I'm creating my own face, my own heart—a Nahuatl concept.

—GLORIA ANZALDÚA, *poet and critic*

The key to the treasure is the treasure.

—JOHN BARTH, *novelist*

Why do I write? Perhaps in order not to go mad.

—ELIE WIESEL, *novelist and essayist*

Imagine straddling the cosmos, clinging to the tails of comets, knowing that time does not exist. That is the writer's life. It is the purest connection to the universe a mortal can have. It is also a kind of prayer.

—ERICA JONG, *poet and novelist*

Index

O

Oates, Joyce Carol, 37, 39
O'Brien, Edna, 14, 107
O'Brien, Meg, 11
O'Connor, Flannery, 20, 22, 27, 30,
    41, 55, 105, 120
Oneal, Zibby, 77, 91
O'Neil, Paul, 16
Orwell, George, 11, 49, 80, 101;
    rejection letter, 95
Oz, Amos, 7, 59, 133
Ozick, Cynthia, 56, 126

P

Paige, Satchel, 112
Paley, Grace, 2, 4, 8, 138
Parker, Dorothy, 118
Parker, Thomas Trebitsch, 72
Parton, Dolly, 16
Paterson, Katherine, 10, 45, 76
Pavarotti, Luciano, 12
Pavese, Cesare, 22
Peacock, Thomas Love, 19
Peck, Richard, 1, 6, 9, 57, 71
Penzler, Otto, 101
Perkins, Lori, 87
Perkins, Maxwell, 16, 71, 90
Phillips, Louis, 84, 125, 127
Picasso, Pablo, 2, 80
Pickford, Mary, 113
Pinker, Steven, 63
Plath, Sylvia, 94
Plotnik, Arthur, 26, 90, 92
Polito, Robert, 5
Pope, Alexander, 33
Porter, Katherine Anne, 64,
    128
Powell, Dawn, 69
Powers, John, 19
Preil, Gabriel, 72, 135
Prelutsky, Jack, 4
Previn, André, 114
Prose, Francine, 24
Proust, Marcel, 48
Provost, Gary, 72
Publishers Weekly, 97

Q

Quindlen, Anna, 111

R

Reid, Alastair, 7
Rich, Adrienne, 105, 114
Riding, Laura, 19
Rilke, Rainer Maria, 63
Robbins, Jerome, 113
Roethke, Theodore, 66
Rogers, Samuel, 27
Rogers, Will, 3
Roosevelt, Eleanor, 113
Roth, Philip, 78
Rousseau, Jean-Jacques, 6
Rudin, Scott, 61
Rukeyser, Muriel, 58
Rushdie, Salman, 49
Ruskin, John, 25
Russell, Bertrand, 106
Rylant, Cynthia, 36

S

Salanter, Israel, 98
Salinger, J. D., 96
Sandburg, Carl, 31
Saroyan, William, 84
Sarton, May, 1
Sayers, Dorothy L., 65
Scheer, George, 100
Schuster, M. Lincoln, 87, 91
Schwartz, Delmore, 36
Schweitzer, Albert, 130
Schweninger, Ann, 131
Scieszka, Jon, 29, 45, 50
Scorsese, Martin, 12
Sendak, Maurice, 6, 34, 124
Settle, Mary Lee, 24
Seuss, Dr., 40, 78
Sexton, Anne, 137
Shange, Ntozake, 2
Shaw, George Bernard, 97, 115
Shaw, Irwin, 115
Shepard, Jim, 29, 115
Shields, Carol, 57, 60